The Three Minds

-From Pain to Power-

Developing Mental Toughness and Overcoming Hurts!

Harrison S Mungal, Ph.D., PsyD

The Three Minds

Copyright © 2024 Harrison S. Mungal

Contact author via email: info@harrisonmungal.com
www.agetoage.ca
www.harrisonmungal.com
www.harrisonmungalbooks.com
Facebook: Harrison Mungal
Twitter: HarrisonandKathleen @HKrelationships
AgetoAge @agetoagec
LinkedIn: Harrison Mungal, Ph.D., PsyD
YouTube: Harrison Mungal
Phone: 905-533-1334

ABOUT *the*
AUTHOR

Harrison Sharma Mungal, BTh, MCC, MSW, PhD, PsyD

Dr. Mungal is a devoted therapist with a background in mental health and clinical psychology, driven by a genuine passion for life and the well-being of those under his care. With an impressive literary portfolio comprising over 40 books and a seasoned public speaking career that has reached audiences in over 42 nations, he brings a wealth of knowledge and skills to his practice.

Alongside his professional accomplishments, Dr. Mungal places a high value on family, with a successful marriage of over 34 years, seven children, and multiple grandchildren. In addition to his clinical practice, Dr. Mungal and his wife have played pivotal roles in church planting, pastoral ministry, and missionary work, even during the challenging times of the Cold War in Croatia from 1994-1997. They have nurtured congregations, established churches, and served as missionaries, demonstrating a deep commitment to spreading the gospel. Their dedication extended to running a Bible college, Metro Bible College, for over a decade before transitioning into mental health and addictions counselling.

Dr. Mungal is widely respected for his unique ability to blend biblical principles with scientific insights, adding a distinctive "psychology twist" to his therapeutic approach. He explained God made us Body, Soul (mind, will and emotions) and Spirit. As much as people need support physically and spiritually, "the soul is where people are wounded and is in need of healing." His expertise has been sought after by various media outlets, including appearances on television programs including 700 Clubs Canada and 100 Huntly St. He has also been invited to speak at prestigious institutions such as the Attorney General of Canada, police departments, hospitals, community agencies, and churches. His contributions have earned him accolades and recognition from local authorities, police departments, mayors, community leaders, and countless families.

With over 21 years of experience in mental health, psychiatry, and psychology, coupled with over four decades dedicated to teaching and preaching the gospel, Dr. Mungal possesses a wealth of expertise in both fields. His educational background is equally impressive, with a Christian Leadership Certificate, a Ministerial Diploma from two years of Bible College, a bachelor's degree in Theology, two master's degrees (in Counselling and Social Work), and two doctorate degrees (in Social Work and Clinical Psychology).

In summary, Dr. Mungal's journey is a testament to his unwavering commitment to serving others, integrating his faith with his professional expertise to make a positive impact in the lives of countless individuals, couples, and families. His multifaceted career reflects a deep sense of purpose and a profound dedication to promoting holistic healing and spiritual growth.

TABLE *Of* CONTENT

INTRODUCTION

Welcome to an exploration of "The Three Minds," a journey that delves into the intricate landscape of our mental world. This book is not just a collection of theories or abstract concepts; it's a practical guide that connects with the everyday experiences we all face. Whether you're looking to master your mind, heal a hurt mind, or understand how our collective minds shape our world, this book offers insights and tools to help you navigate these complexities.

Imagine your mind as a powerful tool, capable of great feats when wielded with skill and care. The first part of our journey is about mastering this tool, understanding how to harness its full potential. It's like learning to drive a car: once you understand how it works and how to control it, you can go anywhere you want. We'll explore practical techniques to develop mental toughness, sharpen focus, and enhance your ability to stay calm under pressure. These skills are not just for those facing extraordinary challenges but are essential for anyone wanting to live a balanced and fulfilling life.

Life throws us all curveballs, and sometimes, these experiences leave us with a hurt mind. Think of it like a wound that needs attention and care. This section is about acknowledging that pain, understanding its impact, and learning how to heal. We'll talk about recognizing when our mind is hurting, the importance of self-care, and strategies for recovery. Healing is a personal journey, and this part of the book is designed to offer support and guidance, helping you find your way back to mental well-being.

We are not just individuals; we are part of a community, a society that shapes and is shaped by the collective mind. This section explores the concept of "our minds" – how our thoughts and actions are influenced by those around us and how we, in turn, impact others. It's like a ripple effect in a pond, where each drop creates waves that touch every part of the water. Understanding this interconnectedness helps us see beyond our personal perspective and appreciate the broader context of our actions. We'll discuss the power of empathy, the importance of connection, and how to cultivate a supportive and understanding environment for ourselves and others.

Mental toughness is the backbone that supports our journey through mastering, healing, and connecting our minds. It's about resilience, the ability to bounce back from setbacks, and the strength to keep going even when things get tough. This part of the book provides practical advice on how to develop and maintain mental toughness, using real-life examples and actionable steps. It's like building muscle; the more you work on it, the stronger it becomes.

As you dive into the chapters ahead, I encourage you to reflect on your own experiences and think about how these concepts apply to your life. The goal of this book is to make the abstract tangible and to provide you with tools that you can use to navigate the complexities of your mind. Whether you are seeking to master your mind, heal from past hurts, or better understand your place in the world, "The Three Minds" offers a path forward. Let's embark on this journey together, and I hope you find it as enlightening and empowering as I have.

This introduction is designed to be engaging and relatable, setting the stage for a book that offers practical insights into understanding and navigating our mental landscape.

THE *Three* MINDS

The power of the human mind is a vast and complex phenomenon that has captivated philosophers, psychologists, and scientists for centuries. It is within the realms of our minds that our thoughts, emotions, and decision-making processes converge, shaping our perceptions of the world and influencing the course of our lives. We need to understand the intricate interplay between the emotional mind, reasonable mind, and wise mind. We need to unravel the distinct aspects of each mind and explore how they contribute to our understanding of ourselves and the world around us.

The human mind is a complex and multifaceted entity that plays a crucial role in our daily lives, including our decision-making processes. To understand the power of the mind, it is important to recognize and unravel its different aspects.

Negotiating with our own minds can often be a challenging endeavour. Our thoughts, emotions, and desires may sometimes pull us in different directions, creating inner conflicts and dilemmas. There is an art of negotiation within our own minds, seeking to find common ground, identify our true values and motivations, and forge a harmonious alliance between the emotional, reasonable, and wise minds.

By understanding and harnessing the power of these different aspects of our minds, we can cultivate greater self-awareness, make more informed decisions, and lead lives that are balanced, fulfilling, and in alignment with our truest selves.

At the core of our mental landscape lies the emotional mind, which serves as a wellspring of feelings, passions, and impulses. Our emotional minds play a significant role in our daily lives, influencing our perceptions, feelings, opinions, actions, and the decisions we make. It can shape our decision-making processes, clouding our judgment or leading us astray, while at other times offering valuable insights and guiding us towards optimal outcomes. Our emotional minds can be viewed as a tomato; it has thin skin and can feel everything including verbal and nonverbal communications from others. This can create issues as we react to how we feel and not considering the logics and facts behind the thought or action taken in making a decision or adding resolutions. Tomatoes are usually juicy and sweet but can be damage very easily.

Our emotional minds are contagious, and the emotions of others can influence our decision making. When we are surrounded by individuals expressing strong emotions, it can affect our own emotional state and consequently impact our choices. For instance, in a group setting, if there is a prevalent sense of enthusiasm for a particular option, we may be more inclined to follow the crowd and make decisions based on the collective emotional atmosphere. It is crucial to recognize this influence and assess whether our decisions align with our individual values and goals.

Our emotion minds can introduce biases into decision making, leading us to favour certain options or perspectives based on our emotional state. For example, if we are feeling anxious or fearful, we may be more likely to choose the safest or most familiar option, even if it is not the most optimal. On the other hand, positive emotions can lead to overconfidence and risk-taking. Being aware of these biases can help us critically evaluate our decisions and consider alternative perspectives.

The emotional minds can be wounded for years if not cared for and not considering the bigger picture in life. If we focus on the negative feeling that comes from its wounds, we will not allow ourselves to be healed. When the emotional mind rules, it is easy for us to react impulsively without thinking of what is being said at the moment. Our primary thought is spoken and not our secondary thought which is our processed thoughts.

Our emotional minds regulation refers to the ability to manage and control our emotions effectively. Making decisions under the influence of intense emotions, such as anger or sadness, can cloud our judgment and lead to impulsive or irrational choices. Developing emotional intelligence and self-awareness allows us to recognize and regulate our emotions, creating a space for more reasoned decision making. It is easy to feel everyone is against us because they did not agree with us. When people agree with us, we see them as friends but that can change from zero to a hundred the moment they disagree. Learning to agree to disagree can be problematic as we have difficult understanding that concept. We need to understand our emotions can be negative but can also be positive. Learning to grow the positive emotional mind can be a struggle, but not impossible.

When faced with a decision, our emotional mind can strongly influence our thought processes and subsequent actions. Our emotions such as fear, anger, or excitement can cloud our judgment and lead us to make impulsive or irrational choices. On the other hand, emotions can also provide valuable insights and intuitive signals about our preferences, values, and desires. It is important to acknowledge and understand our emotions without letting them overpower our reasoning abilities.

The emotional mind can be viewed as part of our consciousness that is driven by emotions, feelings, and desires. It is responsible for our immediate and instinctual reactions to various stimuli. This is one reason why when we live with developing the emotional mind as the dominant mind, we can be hurt easily by what we don't want to hear. We can be easily suicidal or harm ourselves very frequently. We can become sexually active with multiple partners, have difficult making decisions and sees the world as our enemy. We may find it a challenge to take constructive criticism and maintain a stable job as we don't like being told what to do.

The emotional mind is highly influential in decision making as it can colour our perceptions, bias our judgments, and drive impulsive actions. When operating solely from the emotional mind, we may find ourselves making decisions based on temporary emotional states rather than careful consideration. It plays a significant role in the decision-making process, often shaping our perceptions, judgments, and actions (Damasio, A. R., 2020). It is essential to understand how our emotional minds can both enhance and hinder our decision-making abilities.

Our emotional minds can serve as intuitive signals, providing us with valuable information about a situation or person. Our gut feelings and instincts often arise from subconscious processing, integrating past experiences and stored knowledge. While it is important to trust our intuition, it is equally important to balance it with rational analysis. By acknowledging and exploring our intuitive signals, we can gain deeper insights into our decision-making processes.

While our emotional minds can introduce biases, they can

also provide valuable insights into our preferences, values, and desires. Engaging with our emotions allows us to connect with our authentic selves and make decisions that align with our true needs and aspirations. By acknowledging and understanding our emotions, we can integrate them into the decision-making process, using them as a guide rather than letting them dominate our choices.

Recognizing the influence of emotions on decision making is a crucial step towards achieving a balance between the emotional mind and the reasonable mind. By cultivating self-awareness, emotional intelligence, and the ability to regulate our emotions, we can make more informed and balanced decisions. Incorporating both reason and emotions in the decision-making process enables us to tap into the wisdom of the wise mind, leading to outcomes that align with our values and promote overall well-being.

While our emotional minds provide a crucial input, it is essential to recognize the role of logic and rationality in sound decision making. The reasonable mind represents the realm of logical thinking, facts, rationalization, objective analysis, and critical reasoning. This mind can help us evaluate information, weigh the pros and cons, and make informed choices, thereby offering a counterbalance to the sometimes overwhelming influence of emotions.

Balancing our emotional and reasonable minds are crucial for making optimal decisions and achieving favourable outcomes. Both the emotional and reasonable mind play significant roles in our decision-making processes, and finding the right balance between them is essential for making well-informed and thoughtful choices.

The reasonable mind is essential for critical thinking, problem-solving, and weighing the pros and cons of different options. However, when the reasonable mind dominates decision making, it can lead to a lack of empathy or disregard for the emotional impact of choices. This mind are more dominant in most men as they find it difficult to be emotional, especially when emotions was viewed as a sense of weakness.

The reasonable mind can be viewed as a cantaloupe, sweet inside but has a thick skin outside. When this mind dominated a person, they can have difficult relating and connecting to others. They can have insecurities and lack of confidence in themselves, so not sharing their emotions makes them feel safe.

However, achieving optimal outcomes often lies in finding a delicate balance between the emotional and reasonable minds. The ability to integrate and harmonize these two aspects can lead to more nuanced and effective decision making. We need to balance our emotions with rationality, allowing for a more comprehensive understanding of complex situations and fostering the development of optimal solutions.

The reasonable mind play a crucial role in sound decision making. While our emotional minds provide valuable insights and inform our preferences, it is essential to balance them with logical reasoning to make informed choices. By engaging the reasonable mind, we can evaluate situations objectively, consider relevant facts and evidence, and assess the potential outcomes of our decisions.

The reasonable mind guide us in collecting and analysing relevant information before making a decision. We can use critical thinking skills to assess the credibility and reliability of the sources, identify biases, and weigh the evidence. By relying on objective data and facts, we can make decisions based on a solid foundation.

Applying the reasonable mind helps us identify cause and effect relationships within a decision-making context. By understanding the potential consequences of different choices, we can evaluate the long-term implications and consider the ripple effects that each option may have. This analysis allows us to make choices that align with our goals and values.

The reasonable mind enable us to assess the probability and risk associated with different outcomes. By examining the available information, we can estimate the likelihood of various scenarios and consider the potential benefits and drawbacks of each. This evaluation allows us to make more calculated decisions, weighing the potential rewards against the associated risks.

Cognitive biases are inherent tendencies that can lead to irrational decision making. By engaging the reasonable mind, we can recognize and mitigate these biases. Logical reasoning helps us identify when our thinking might be influenced by cognitive biases such as confirmation bias (favouring information that confirms pre-existing beliefs) or anchoring bias (relying too heavily on initial information). By consciously challenging these biases, we can make more objective decisions.

Deductive reasoning involves drawing specific conclusions from general principles, while inductive reasoning involves forming general principles based on specific observations. Both forms of reasoning can be valuable in decision making. Deductive reasoning allows us to apply existing knowledge and rules to reach logical conclusions, while inductive reasoning allows us to form hypotheses and generate new insights. By employing these forms of reasoning, we can think systematically and consider multiple perspectives.

The reasonable mind helps us weigh the pros and cons of different options. By objectively evaluating the advantages and disadvantages of each alternative, we can identify the potential benefits and drawbacks associated with them. This process enables us to make more informed decisions that align with our goals and values.

The reasonable mind encourages us to consider the long-term implications of our decisions. It helps us think beyond immediate gratification or short-term gains and consider the impact of our choices on our future well-being. By aligning our decisions with our long-term goals, we can make choices that promote our overall growth and fulfilment.

Engaging in the reasonable mind involves seeking input and feedback from others. By considering different perspectives and inviting diverse opinions, we can enhance the quality of our decision making. Rationality allows us to objectively evaluate the input received, weigh its relevance, and integrate it into our decision-making process.

By recognizing the importance of the reasonable mind and bringing a balance with the emotional mind, we can leverage these cognitive tools to make more sound and informed decisions. Embracing the reasonable mind alongside the emotional and wise minds allows us to achieve a balanced approach, considering both the facts and our emotional responses. Ultimately, this integration leads to decisions that are not only well-reasoned but also aligned with our values, emotions, and long-term goals.

To strike a balance between our emotional and reasonable minds, it is essential to develop self-awareness and introspection. Being aware of our emotional state and its potential impact on decision making allows us to take a step back and assess the situation more objectively. Mindfulness practices can be immensely helpful in cultivating this self-awareness and reducing impulsive reactions driven solely by emotions.

An effective strategy for balancing our emotional and reasonable minds is to acknowledge and validate our emotions while also subjecting them to critical scrutiny. This involves acknowledging and understanding the emotions we experience, recognizing their influence on our thoughts and actions, and then critically evaluating whether these emotions align with the logical aspects of the decision at hand.

For instance, if you are considering a job offer that excites you, it is important to acknowledge and appreciate the positive emotions associated with it. However, it is equally important to evaluate the practical aspects, such as whether the job aligns with your long-term goals, offers a favourable work-life balance, and provides adequate financial stability. By objectively assessing both emotional and rational factors, you can make a more balanced and informed decision.

In some cases, our emotional and reasonable minds may appear to be in conflict, pulling us in different directions. In such situations, it can be helpful to seek additional information, advice, or perspectives from trusted individuals. Engaging in open and honest discussions with others can provide valuable insights and help us gain a broader understanding of the situation, enabling us to find a more harmonious balance between emotions and reason.

Ultimately, achieving a balance between our emotional and reasonable minds requires practice and conscious effort. It involves recognizing the strengths and limitations of both aspects and finding ways to integrate them effectively. By acknowledging our emotions, harnessing the power of reason, and subjecting our decisions to thoughtful analysis, we can make more well-rounded choices that align with our values, goals, and overall well-being.

Remember that finding the right balance between emotions and reason is a dynamic process, and it may vary depending on the context and nature of the decision. With time and practice, you can develop the ability to navigate the complexities of decision making, tapping into both the emotional and rational aspects of your mind to achieve optimal outcomes.

The wise mind encompasses a harmonious integration of both the emotional and reasonable minds. It is a state of balanced decision making that combines the wisdom of emotions with the clarity of rationality. The wise mind involves accessing our intuition, inner wisdom, and deeper understanding of ourselves and the situation at hand. When we tap into the wise mind, we make decisions that align with our values, consider the emotions of ourselves and others, and take into account the long-term consequences.

Beyond the emotional and reasonable minds lies the concept of the wise mind, which represents the synthesis of intuition, insight, and deep understanding. The wise mind draws upon the wisdom of our experiences, the integration of our emotional and rational faculties, and a profound sense of self-awareness. We will explore how cultivating the wise mind can enhance our decision-making capabilities and lead to outcomes that are aligned with our values, aspirations, and long-term well-being.

Understanding these different aspects of the mind is crucial because it allows us to recognize the strengths and limitations of each. By becoming aware of how our emotions and reasoning influence our decision making, we can cultivate a greater sense of self-awareness and make more informed choices.

The wise mind play a significant role in decision making, complementing the rational and logical aspects of the mind. While our emotional and reasonable minds have their place, intuition offers a unique perspective that can lead to innovative solutions and successful outcomes. This can be considered the wise mind. When our emotional and reasonable minds are combined and balanced together, we can grow the wise mind.

Integrating the wise mind into decision-making processes involves tapping into your subconscious knowledge and relying on your instincts. We can then harness what is best for us, others and integrate effective decision making for the future.

The wise mind can be described as a deep, instinctual understanding that arises without conscious reasoning. It involves accessing information and patterns that may not be immediately evident to the conscious mind. Intuitive insights often manifest as sudden "aha" moments, strong feelings, or a sense of certainty. While intuition is difficult to define and quantify, it is a valuable tool that can guide decision-making processes.

The wise mind are visceral responses that emerge from our core being. They can be described as a "knowing" or a strong sensation that something is right or wrong. These feelings are often tied to our body's physiological responses, such as a quickening heartbeat or a tightening sensation in the stomach. Trusting our gut feelings means paying attention to these bodily sensations and acknowledging them as valuable inputs in the decision-making process.

The wise mind should not be seen as a replacement for rationality and logic but rather as a complement to them. Striking a balance between intuition and rationality involves considering both aspects when making decisions. While rationality provides a systematic and analytical approach, the wise mind can offer a broader perspective that takes into account subtle cues and subconscious knowledge. By integrating the two, we can arrive at more holistic and well-informed decisions.

Developing the wise mind requires cultivating self-awareness and practicing mindfulness. By becoming more attuned to our thoughts, feelings, and bodily sensations, we can gain insights into our intuitive processes. Regular meditation and mindfulness exercises can help us quiet the noise of the conscious mind and tap into our wise mind. Additionally, paying attention to past experiences and reflecting on instances when our wise mind proved accurate, can help build trust in our intuitive abilities.

While the wise mind can be a powerful tool, it is important

to validate and test our insights when making important decisions. This can involve gathering additional information, seeking diverse perspectives, or conducting experiments to confirm or refute our intuitive hunches. By combining intuitive insights with evidence-based reasoning, we can make more robust decisions and minimize the risk of being swayed solely by emotions or biases.

The wise mind often thrives in situations that require creative problem-solving and innovation. By embracing the wise mind, we open ourselves up to novel ideas, alternative perspectives, and unconventional solutions. This can be particularly valuable in complex and ambiguous situations where relying solely on rationality may not lead to optimal outcomes. The wise mind can help us think outside the box and consider possibilities that may have been overlooked by a purely analytical approach.

Developing the wise mind is a crucial aspect of harnessing the power of our minds. It enables us to adapt to changing circumstances, navigate complex challenges, and generate innovative solutions. The wise mind includes embracing diverse perspectives, questioning assumptions, and embracing uncertainty, as we strive for better problem-solving abilities.

Developing the wise mind is a crucial skill for better problem-solving, as it allows individuals to adapt their thinking and approach to different situations. Understanding the concept of the wise mind is the first step towards developing this skill. It involves the ability to shift between different the emotional and reasonable mind, such as feelings, attention, perception, facts, logics and rationalizations and problem-solving strategies, in response to changing circumstances.

To enhance the wise mind it is important to adopt a growth mindset. Believing that your abilities and intelligence can be developed through effort and learning allows you to approach problems with a more open and flexible mindset. Embracing a growth mindset encourages you to seek out challenges and view setbacks as opportunities for growth, which in turn enhances your ability to adapt and find creative solutions.

Another effective way to enhance the wise mind is by embracing novel experiences. Engaging in activities that expose you to new information, ideas, and perspectives can broaden your thinking and stimulate cognitive flexibility. This can involve reading diverse books, exploring different cultures, learning new skills, or engaging in creative hobbies. By exposing yourself to a variety of experiences, you expand your mental repertoire and become more adaptable in your thinking.

Practicing perspective-taking is another valuable strategy for the development of the wise mind. By actively putting yourself in someone else's shoes and considering alternative viewpoints, you develop a greater understanding of different perspectives and increase your capacity to consider a wider range of solutions to problems. This exercise allows you to break free from rigid thinking patterns and encourages you to explore new possibilities.

Engaging in intellectually challenging activities is also beneficial for developing the wise mind. Puzzles, brainteasers, strategy games, and other mentally stimulating tasks require you to think critically, analyse situations from different angles, and adapt your approach based on new information. These activities train your brain to be more flexible and adaptable in problem-solving situations.

Being comfortable with uncertainty and ambiguity is another important aspect of the wise mind. Embracing the unknown allows you to explore new possibilities and consider alternative solutions. Recognizing that not all problems have clear-cut answers and that there can be multiple paths to reach a solution frees you from rigid thinking and encourages more innovative problem-solving.

Challenging your assumptions and beliefs is also essential for developing the wise mind. By questioning your own preconceived notions, you open yourself up to new ideas and perspectives. This mindset shift can lead to more creative problem-solving and the discovery of alternative solutions that you may not have considered before.

Practicing divergent thinking is another effective way to grow the wise mind. Divergent thinking involves generating multiple creative solutions to a problem. Engaging in brainstorming exercises or creative activities that encourage you to think beyond conventional boundaries expands the wise mind and encourages you to consider a wide range of possibilities. This approach allows for more innovative problem-solving and helps overcome mental rigidity.

When it comes to decision-making, we often find ourselves in a constant internal negotiation between our emotional mind, reasonable mind, and wise mind. These three aspects of the mind represent different perspectives and influences that shape our choices and actions. Negotiating with your own mind involves finding a harmonious balance between these three aspects to make informed and well-rounded decisions.

To begin the process of negotiating with your own mind, it's important to cultivate self-awareness. This means recognizing and acknowledging your emotional responses, thoughts, and biases that may influence your decision-making. By understanding your own mental states, you can better navigate through conflicting emotions and thoughts that may arise during the decision-making process.

One key aspect of negotiating with your own mind is the ability to differentiate between the emotional and reasonable mind. The emotional mind can provide valuable insights and guide us towards what matters most to us, but they can also cloud our judgment and lead to impulsive decisions. The reasonable mind, on the other hand, emphasizes logic, facts, and objective analysis. By acknowledging the role of both the emotional and reasonable minds, we can strive for a balanced approach that takes into account both the heart and the mind.

To negotiate effectively with your own mind, it is crucial to develop emotional intelligence. Emotional intelligence involves recognizing, understanding, and managing your own emotions, as well as empathizing with the emotions of others. By honing your emotional intelligence, you can navigate through difficult emotions, such as fear or anger, and make decisions that are not solely driven by intense emotional reactions.

Furthermore, integrating the wise mind into the decision-making process is essential. While logic and reasoning play a significant role, our wise mind provide valuable insights that go beyond rational analysis. The wise mind is often based on subconscious processing of information and can provide a holistic understanding of a situation. By listening to your wise mind and combining it with rational thinking, you can tap into a deeper level of wisdom and make more holistic decisions.

The wise mind is crucial for negotiating with your own minds. This gives you the ability to adapt your thinking, perspectives, and strategies when faced with new information or changing circumstances. By being open-minded and willing to consider alternative viewpoints, you can challenge your own preconceptions and expand your range of possibilities. The wise mind helps you avoid getting stuck in rigid thinking patterns and enables you to explore creative solutions to problems.

Remember, integrating the wise mind into decision making is not about dismissing rationality or emotions, but about harnessing the collective power of the emotional mind, reasonable mind, and wise mind. By acknowledging and embracing all these aspects of our minds, we can achieve a harmonious and balanced approach to decision making, leading to more satisfying and successful outcomes.

Developing the ability to navigate between the emotional, reasonable, and wise minds is a skill that can be honed through practice. It requires cultivating emotional intelligence, enhancing cognitive flexibility, and nurturing mindfulness. The ultimate goal is to find harmony and balance within these aspects of the mind, allowing us to make decisions that are both emotionally satisfying and logically sound.

To find harmony and balance within these three aspects of the mind, it is important to cultivate self-awareness and mindfulness. By practicing self-reflection, we can observe our thoughts, emotions, and reasoning patterns. This awareness enables us to recognize when one aspect of our mind is overpowering the others and adjust accordingly. Mindfulness helps us stay present in the moment, allowing us to make conscious choices rather than being driven solely by impulsive emotions or detached reason.

Ultimately, finding harmony and balance within the emotional, reasonable, and wise minds is an ongoing process. It requires practice, self-reflection, and a commitment to personal growth. When we achieve this balance, we become more aligned with our authentic selves and make decisions that reflect our true values and aspirations. By integrating all aspects of our mind, we unlock our full potential and create a life that is both fulfilling and purposeful.

In conclusion, exploring the power of the mind and understanding its different aspects can greatly enhance our decision-making abilities and overall well-being. Throughout this chapter, we have delved into the intricate workings of the emotional mind, the reasonable mind, and the wise mind. By unravelling these distinct facets, we have gained valuable insights into how our thoughts, emotions, and reasoning processes influence our choices and actions.

Negotiating with our own minds is an art that requires patience, self-compassion, and practice. Recognizing when our emotional mind or our reasonable mind dominates our decision-making process empowers us to consciously shift our focus and tap into the wisdom of the wise mind. It is through this negotiation that we find alignment and synergy within ourselves, facilitating more harmonious and balanced decision-making.

Understanding the power of the mind involves unravelling its various aspects and embracing the interplay between the emotional mind, reasonable mind, and wise mind. By recognizing the influence of our emotions, incorporating logical thinking, integrating intuition, cultivating cognitive flexibility, and negotiating with ourselves, we can achieve harmony and balance within our decision-making process. With this awareness and skill set, we are better equipped to navigate the complexities of life, make choices that align with our values, and ultimately foster personal growth and well-being.

MASTER *the* MIND

The mind is the most powerful gift we were created with, along with the heart, and if we don't use our minds correctly, it can be highly destructive. The thoughts flowing through our minds can be a blessing or a curse. The thoughts we entertain affect our perception and how we interpret information. We all struggle from time to time with our complex thinking patterns. However, with the help of divergent thinking, we can set our minds free.

We need to let our thoughts flow smoothly but should not allow them to rule us. Our thoughts can run wildly if we do not take control of them. Controlling our thoughts is like raising children. If we don't master parenting, our children will walk all over us. They will then bring shame and disrespect upon themselves and their families.

Similarly, lacking control over the mind will bring negative consequences. Unwanted thoughts that reside in our minds will create unproductive and unhealthy thinking. Changing our thinking to dispel such thoughts will eventually allow us to control our behaviours.

Mastering the mind involves managing the thoughts that flow through the mind. It involves reprogramming our thinking. This takes skill, and any talent must be developed. Mastering the mind is like mastering a career or hobby, except the mind is with us twenty-four-seven.

Learning a language takes time, regardless of who we are and what culture or ethnic background we are from. Speaking a language with the perfect dialect takes much effort and experience. Similarly, we can master our minds with the same principles. The more effort we give, the less stressful we will be in the process. Everything in life takes time to master, like a language. The more we practice speaking it, the more fluent it becomes.

There are many thoughts that take up a lot of space in our brains, like "squatters" who do not have permission to live in the location they choose. Some of our thoughts are there in our minds not because we have consciously given permission but because they came along due to past hurts. The more they are fed with negativity, the more control they have, and eventually, they rule the mind just like a squatter who will take over land or a residence they reside in. In order to take charge, make sure you are the one consciously permitting these thoughts to stay in your mind; otherwise, dispel them.

There is usually a loose conglomeration of thoughts running through our minds that come from words spoken to us as children. It is often the case that these words take up space in our minds. These are usually thoughts that have us comparing ourselves with others, believing that we are useless, feeling that we will never succeed, or constantly in a state of trying to fulfill other people's expectations of us. The conglomeration of thoughts that come from rejection and betrayal, which creates emotional pain, should be discarded ceremoniously, like putting an object that represents negativity in a box and burying or burning it. These are the thoughts that cripple us, and instead of being a master of our minds, we become a slave to them.

We should never allow our thoughts to make us feel like we are in bondage or like we are a slave to fear and worry. Anger, frustration, emotional pain, and regrets grow when we live in bondage. A lack of motivation, low self-esteem, insecurity, anxiety, depression, passivity, and violent behaviours are all signs that we may be in bondage due to our thoughts. Despite how much effect our thoughts can have on us, we are the masters of what we think. We need to stop ourselves from thinking negatively. Start by saying to yourself, "I am in control." We can actually write it down or print on paper "I am in control" and paste it in places where it is visible to remind ourselves, we are in charge of ourselves. We should not blame others for our behaviours and actions.

We need to avoid is beating ourselves up. It is okay to admit our flaws, weaknesses, faults ad regrets, but we need to move on. Don't allow thoughts of self-disappointment to stay in your brain. No one can change what has happened; however, we can problem-solve. Therefore, looking for solutions instead of allowing negative thoughts to rule our minds should be our focus when things do not go the way we want them to. Sometimes we are our worst bullies. Don't allow your mind to bully you with negative thoughts.

Some unanswered questions that may help you and that are usually asked. "What are some tricks and pointers to becoming masters of your minds?" "How do we get rid of the slave mentality?" "How do we take charge of our thinking?"

Most of us need to change our attitude toward ourselves and others, at least at some point in our lives. We need to come to a place in life where we can conclude we don't have all the answers to all of life's problems, and we cannot "fix" others who may have wronged us. Let that new positive attitude extend even to our enemies. When we start living in this fashion, we will grasp the basics of mastering our minds.

We should be alert to opportunities, realize that opportunities may never come again, and take advantage of them when they are in our hands. We may fail, but that's a risk we will have to take. Each failure will draw us closer to the prize. Opportunities will expand our experience and develop our skill set.

We need to accept people for who they are instead of trying to change them to be us. We all do our own assessment of people we meet and make a conscious decision to engage with them or maintain a distance. Accepting the fact that we cannot change anyone, but we can work with them is another skill we need in order to master the mind. We can give suggestions and recommendations but cannot make someone become the person we want. A great deal of anxiety comes from feeling a lack of control when people do not behave how we want them to. People may even do things that can negatively influence us. Learning to accept others while being yourself and to let them make their own choices will have a positive impact on your relationship with them which in turn will positively impact your outlook.

When we take responsibility, we set a different new example in life. We create a blueprint for others to follow. Regardless of what issues may arise as a result of our participation, we need to learn to take responsibility. We could be 100% right or 100% wrong, but we should take responsibility for finding a solution rather than blaming others. This shows maturity, but it is also a trick to allowing ourselves to learn that we are a master of our lives. So many of us live our lives more or less by ourselves and fail to include others.

We need to ask ourselves why? Where did it stem from? We can socialize and engage with others and not allow the power of influence to affect us. We can be in control of our minds and what we think of ourselves and others without allowing fear to control us. We were created to be among others to help with healthy stimulants, which assist with preventative factors that will affect our mental health long term.

We need to maintain a mind of a student. Some of us may give the impression that we know it all and that we have an answer for everything in life, yet our own lives are falling apart. It is only to compensate for self-perceived or actual incompetence. We can learn on a daily basis from other people around us. We may learn minor things or get major revelations, but when we are willing to learn, we will always be one step closer to mastering what we are learning. Assuming the role of a student allows for new thoughts to replace discarded thoughts as we stay in control of what we allow into our minds.

We also need to maintain a mind of a teacher. One thing observed from teaching is that it forces you to learn. When time is spent preparing a lesson, knowledge is gained. And, when we teach, experience and skills are sharpened. Being a teacher sometimes forces us to take control of what we are saying and how we are saying it to ensure that others receive our message effectively. Find out how we can speak into the lives of others, even if it's our loved ones. The concept of centring our thoughts around communicating a theme will help us in taking control of our thought life.

When the brain is "infected," things can go awry, and the brain no longer serves its purpose efficiently. Symptoms of thought disorders will result as the brain can no longer "carry a conversation" that is sensible. Our brain is a miracle in how it functions, as it holds more information than we could ever imagine. It houses resources we can tap into in the future in an orderly fashion which enables us to perform various impressive tasks. Think of the first time you tried riding a bike. Your brain needs to recall many thoughts in order to keep the bike upright, and it does not matter how many years later you will still know how to ride a bike.

We can become great servants to our minds if we fail to become masters over them. We may find ourselves feeling we cannot control what we think, do, or say, but it is possible with proper discipline. Spend time concentrating and thinking through your thoughts before acting, forming opinions, or communicating opinions. We need to learn how to filter our thoughts if we want to master them.

Mastering our minds draws us closer to the destinies assigned to us. We need to come to a place where we can master our minds. Otherwise, we will never be at peace with ourselves. We need to control what goes into our minds. If it's not good for you, cut it out; otherwise, it will become like cancer and can destroy you. Our thoughts are based on the five sensory systems, which are the precursors to our emotions and the actions we take. Mastering our minds will help us to manage the thoughts that play in our minds, affecting how we feel, what we do, and what comes out of our mouths.

We should never ignore our "gut feeling." Many times before we feed our thought, we have a "gut feeling" that we ignore. If you don't feel good about something, don't pursue it. Sometimes it could be something simple like going over to visit a friend. You are aware your friend is into things you have been working on in your personal life (drinking alcohol, using street drugs, pornography, video games, and so on). You are aware every time you visit your friend; you end up doing things you should not do. If you have a "gut feeling," ignore it and put a sense of peace to the warning thoughts by exploring all the things that can go wrong. Be alert and aware. Many of us usually get trapped into deciding against our "gut feeling" and have regrets.

Some of the choices we make trigger our past, creating more psychological issues affecting our mental health. When we develop unhealthy coping strategies, they can become our default mode to cope when under stress. The mind will lead you to fall into old habits. However, when we master our mind, we can choose alternatives that are new which we can set as new default modes. The healthy neuropathways. An example would be someone who used to use alcohol to cope. The individual may choose to drink club soda with a lime or lemon to avoid drinking alcohol, especially at family events. It is a parallelism to the old pathway. Some individuals may choose to set themselves to have one drink which is monitored by their spouse or family member, as a healthy way to drink alcohol, which is another parallelism. Street drugs, misuse of prescription medications, gambling, and other addictions are considered unhealthy copying strategies which need new healthy parallelism to cope with life's stressors.

We need to learn to say 'No.' The desire to say "no" when we have all intentions to say "yes ." If we yield ourselves to what is being asked that is not in our favour, it may lead us to fall into a trap that stimulates negative thoughts. Learning to say "no" is okay, and that is one thought we should have flowing in our minds. Some people say yes all the time, working all types of extra shifts, helping others move, going to different functions when asked, making donations to everyone who asks, buying items when on sale, buying from door-to-door sellers, going to their friend's sports games, and so on. Learning to say no will help to stay focused on what is most important. Learning to prioritize what is most important will help to become more progressive in life. And this will be another perfect example of mastering the mind when not driven by impulsivity.

We need to control our assumptions as they can condition the mind to carry the wrong message. Controlling our thoughts from the assumption of what is being texted, emailed, or on the phone. So many times, we make a presumption as to what we read, not knowing the full story or the content of what is being written. Some people may have difficulty expressing themselves over the phone by texting and emailing. Developing a thought which is usually negative about a phone call, a text, or an email will play in your mind like a movie. The best is face-to-face or making sure you understand the person you are communicating with before you allow your thought to create a conclusion. It's easy to create thoughts, but they can be very challenging to get rid of.

We need to control planting negative thoughts since they are like weeds that can take over our minds from the fruitfulness of being or staying positive. How many of us try to convince others to like what we like or steer a conversation for others to adapt or engage in? We then become frustrated when the conversation is not going the way we assumed in our minds. We try to make our only conclusion about what the other person's reaction is, what they may say, their mood, how they dress, and their non-verbal language. We try to control others by how we carry on a conversation and not monitoring that we are the dominant ones in the conversation. We speak words to stir the person's emotion or awaken their thoughts, especially if we know some of their weakness or what they have an interest in. We try to live like sales' people, sharing our thoughts to get others to share and then plant our thought seeds into their minds.

Some of us hide our insecurity by speaking negatively about everyone. We have nothing good to say and allow our thoughts that are being created to be negative. Everyone we speak with; we speak to them about someone else. We only see negative attributes, and nothing positive comes out of our month. We may not see it, and the people we associate with it would not say anything since they want to hear the gossip. Although they are aware that the person who is speaking negatively is also speaking negatively about them behind their back, they continue to feed the person's ego. Negativity feeds on your life and will draw joy from your heart. It's better to walk away and refocus your thoughts on something healthy for the mind.

We have the ability to be resilient. This means we can train our minds to stay positive even as we develop our dreams, set goals for our lives, work on plans, and stay on track. We are in control of our thoughts and can do whatever we put our minds to do. We have more control over our thoughts than we may give ourselves credit for. We need to utilize the power of our thought to change the world around us.

With that being said, we need to manage our impulsivity in making decisions, responding to conversations, buying things, and voicing our opinions, especially when we were not asked to share them. Some of us can be impulsive and have an automatic reaction when others speak to us. It's as if someone were to attempt to hit us, and we block ourselves from being hurt. We have an automatic reaction in which, at times, we can say things that can be offensive toward others and bring emotional harm to ourselves. We need to learn how to manage these automatic thoughts and allow our emotional skills to be thicker than tomato skin. We all need to consider how we should respond to others if they enforce their thoughts on us. What would be your reaction, and how would you psychologically deal with it? Some of us can be defensive with what we say, harsh, cold, emotionless, and unrealistic. We need to consider what we give out, and others will react the same and lash back. We all need to learn to be realistic in how we behave with what we say. We should ask ourselves, "is it logical?" "Are we watching the tone of our voices?" Are we being "black and white" in our conversation, not willing to listen to those who are in the grey?" "Are we being mindful that others may have value in what they are saying as much as what we say?"

We need to learn how to be our defence lawyers and cross-exam ourselves to ensure that we are accommodating others as much as we want others to accommodate us. Learning the process of how we think and what we may need to change to associate with others is important. Otherwise, we may live with a delusion that others want to be in our presence when in reality, they are afraid of telling us the truth about how they feel about us. We need to learn to recognize our limitations and speak to others with an understanding that we can make mistakes and are open to corrections. We need to acknowledge that others have tons of value to add to the conversation. We will carry on a long conversation without making others feel they are walking on eggshells. This is a good sign that we are mastering our minds and taking control of our thoughts.

We need to learn that some things we think we need to put on the shelf, especially if they become an obstacle in our relationships with others. Learning that our mind can think faster than we can comprehend and the need not to act on what we think at times is healthy. Mastering the mind gives us that power to be in control, especially when we can remind ourselves that we don't have to give an answer to every question, we don't have to react to every emotion from others, we don't have to be impulsive, and that time is our best friend. We can always give an answer when the dust settles, and we give ourselves some time to process a conversation that may be tense. Mastering the mind is being able to weed out anything that may come across as harmful, demanding, questioning, parenting, and objective.

A HURT MIND

We all inevitably encounter a hurt mind with emotional hurts from a negative past that leaves lasting scars. These wounds can stem from various sources, including abuses, traumas, addictions, dysfunctional families, toxic relationships, abusive relationships, regrets, mistakes, and wrongdoing. They can shape our perspectives, influence our behaviours, and hinder our ability to create a happy future. However, it is within our power to break free from the chains of the past and embrace a transformative process of letting go.

We acknowledge and release emotional hurts when we can explore the profound impact these hurts can have on our well-being, relationships, and personal growth. By understanding the significance of letting go, we can embark on a journey of healing and liberation.

We must navigate the depths of past wounds, including infidelity, mistakes, and the consequences of wrongdoing. By addressing the heavy burden of abuse and trauma, and the weight of bad habits and negative behaviours, we can excel in the destiny for our futures. Practical insights, strategies, and techniques empower us to let go of the pain, reclaim our power, and forge a path toward a brighter future.

Letting go does not mean forgetting or denying the past. It is an act of courage and self-compassion, allowing us to release the emotional baggage that holds us back from experiencing true joy and fulfillment. We need to explore the transformative power of forgiveness, the art of detachment, and the liberation that comes with releasing resentment.

We are never alone with emotional wounds and baggage's. Regardless of our background or experiences, we all must reclaim our lives and pursue a future filled with happiness and self-discovery.

Our memory from the past lingers in our minds, influencing our thoughts, emotions, and behaviours. Emotional hurts from our past have the power to affect our present well-being. We need to embark on the exploration, seek to understand the profound impact of emotional hurts, and how we can move on with our lives.

Imagine carrying a heavy backpack filled with stones collected over the years. Each stone represents a painful experience, a hurtful word spoken, or a traumatic event endured. As you go about your daily life, this burden weighs you down, draining your energy and affecting your every step. These emotional hurts are the stones in your backpack, influencing how you perceive yourself, others, and the world around you. We have a choice to empty the bag or carry it with us.

The impact of these hurts is far-reaching. They shape the lens through which we view ourselves and our capabilities. They can erode our self-esteem, causing us to doubt our worth and potential. The weight of emotional hurts can cloud our judgment, leading us to make choices based on fear, mistrust, or self-doubt rather than from a place of confidence and authenticity. Moreover, these hurts can ripple through our relationships. They can create barriers to intimacy, making it difficult to trust others and form deep disconnections. They can manifest as patterns of withdrawing emotionally or lashing out defensively, which can strain relationships and perpetuate cycles of hurt.

Furthermore, the impact of emotional hurts extends beyond our inner world. They can affect our physical health, as stress and unresolved emotions take a toll on our bodies. They can dampen our enthusiasm, robbing us of the joy and vitality that should accompany each new day. Emotional hurts can even hinder our ability to pursue our dreams and embrace new opportunities, trapping us in a cycle of fear and self-limitation.

By understanding the impact of these emotional hurts, we gain the power to change their influence on our lives. It starts with acknowledging the weight we carry and recognizing that these hurts are not our fault but the result of circumstances and experiences. We can unravel the threads of pain, one by one, and bring them into the light of our awareness. In doing so, we reclaim our power to heal.

We can seek support from trusted friends, family, or professionals who guide and empathize along the journey. We can explore therapeutic techniques, such as journaling, mindfulness, or expressive arts, that allow us to process and release these emotional hurts in a safe and healthy way.

Remember that the impact of emotional hurts is not a life sentence. We have the resiliency within us to overcome our influence and create a brighter future. By exploring the effects of past wounds on our present well-being, we take the first courageous step toward healing and liberation.

We unravel the complexities of emotional hurts, gain insight into their effects, and discover the transformative power of letting go. We are not alone in this pursuit, and as we delve deeper, we can find the strength and wisdom to release the weight of the past and embrace a future filled with joy, fulfillment, and self-discovery.

The impact of emotional hurts often is elusive with powerful emotion of resentment. Resentment can be like a dormant volcano, silently simmering beneath the surface, waiting to erupt and engulf us in its fiery grip. We need to be mindful that we can avoid being resentful for past emotional wounds.

Imagine for a moment that you're holding a magnifying glass, examining the intricate details of your past experiences. As you explore, you will uncover hidden pockets of resentment silently festering over time. These pockets are remnants of unresolved emotions stemming from moments when you felt wronged, betrayed, or undervalued.

Resentment can take various forms. It may arise from a hurtful comment that struck a chord deep within you, a betrayal that shattered your trust, or an injustice that left you feeling powerless. It can be directed towards others, yourself, or even life itself. Whatever the source, these unresolved emotions have the power to shape your perceptions and affect your present well-being.

Unaddressed resentment can become toxic, poisoning our thoughts, emotions, and relationships. It can create a barrier to forgiveness, compassion, and genuine connection. It can also lead to patterns of self-sabotage, where we unknowingly push away opportunities for growth and happiness due to an underlying resentment.

When we uncover hidden resentment, we gain the opportunity to address and release its hold on our lives. This process begins with courageous introspection as we reflect on past experiences and honestly acknowledge the resentment that may have taken root within us.

By shining a light on these hidden pockets of resentment, we allow ourselves to examine them from a place of compassion and understanding. We can explore the underlying causes and triggers, understanding that our emotions are valid and deserving of attention. This process is not about blaming or seeking revenge; it is about taking responsibility for our emotional well-being and finding a path toward healing.

Addressing unresolved resentment requires a combination of self-reflection and seeking support. It may involve engaging in honest conversations with those involved and expressing our feelings in a healthy and assertive manner. It may also involve seeking guidance from a therapist or counsellor who can provide valuable insights and tools for navigating this complex emotional terrain.

Addressing hidden resentment is an act of self-empowerment. It is an acknowledgment that we deserve to live free from unresolved emotions. Uncovering and addressing these hidden pockets of resentment creates space for forgiveness, compassion, and personal growth.

Forgiveness is an integral aspect of releasing the weight of past emotional hurts. Imagine carrying a heavy bag of resentment. Within it lie unresolved emotions, simmering beneath the surface, festering over time. These hidden resentments can quietly erode our well-being, poisoning our thoughts and emotions. They hold us captive, preventing us from fully embracing the present and moving forward with clarity and freedom.

Forgiveness is not about condoning or forgetting the pain we have experienced. It is a transformative act of compassion and self-empowerment, allowing us to release the grip of bitterness and find inner peace.

By forgiving, we are not absolving others of their actions or denying the impact of their hurtful behaviour. Instead, forgiveness grants us the opportunity to reclaim our power and choose a different path. It is an act of liberation from the past, a conscious decision to no longer allow the actions of others to define our present and future.

Forgiveness is not always easy, and it is a deeply personal process. It requires us to face our pain head-on, to acknowledge the depth of our emotions and the wounds inflicted upon us. It may involve reflecting on our role and acknowledging our imperfections. It asks us to summon empathy for ourselves and those who have hurt us, recognizing that we are all flawed and capable of causing harm.

As we embark on the path of forgiveness, we must also uncover the hidden resentments that lie dormant within us. These unresolved emotions can be like buried landmines, triggered by seemingly insignificant events and wreaking havoc on our well-being. By shining a light on these resentments, we give ourselves permission to heal and process the emotions that have been locked away for far too long.

Identifying and addressing these unresolved emotions is a courageous act of self-awareness. It may require us to revisit painful memories to confront the darkness within. But in doing so, we create space for healing and growth. We can seek support through therapy, counselling, or the guidance of trusted individuals who can provide us with tools and perspectives to navigate this complex terrain.

We embark on a transformative journey through forgiveness and uncovering hidden resentments. We free ourselves from the burden of the past, releasing the weight that has held us back from fully embracing the present and the opportunities that lie before us. The journey requires strength, vulnerability, and compassion, but the rewards are immeasurable.

Just as an artist skillfully releases their creation into the world, we, too, have the power to release the grip of past pain that weighs us down. Some techniques and strategies help detach from the shackles of emotional hurts. Letting go is always a challenging task. It requires courage, self-compassion, and a willingness to embrace change. It begins with acknowledging that clinging onto past pain only perpetuates our suffering. We must recognize that holding onto grievances and resentments serves no purpose other than keeping us locked in a cycle of unhappiness.

We need to cultivate a non-judgmental awareness of our thoughts and emotions. We can observe the pain as it arises without getting entangled in its grip. We learn to create space between ourselves and our past hurts, allowing them to exist without defining us. Our perspectives need to be reframed. We can choose to view our experiences not as wounds that define us but as lessons that shape us. By shifting our narrative from victimhood to empowerment, we reclaim our strength in rewriting our story. This reframing process allows us to detach from the pain and see it as a stepping stone toward growth and resilience.

Self-compassion is essential in extending kindness and understanding to ourselves. As we navigate the complexities of letting go, it is essential to acknowledge that healing takes time and that setbacks are a natural part of the process. By treating ourselves with gentleness and patience, we foster an environment of self-nurturing that supports our healing and liberation.

As mentioned before, forgiveness has the power to transmute pain into healing. It is not about condoning or forgetting what has happened but rather about freeing ourselves from the emotional burden that comes with holding onto grudges. Forgiveness is a path to healing, a journey toward inner peace.

Imagine extending a hand of kindness and understanding to yourself, just as you would to a dear friend in pain. That is the essence of self-compassion and forgiveness. It involves treating yourself with love, care, and acceptance, especially when facing emotional challenges or grappling with the impact of past hurts. Self-compassion is a powerful antidote to self-blame, self-criticism, and the relentless pursuit of perfection.

When we experience emotional hurts, it is all too common to berate ourselves, believing that we should have done something differently or are somehow unworthy of healing and happiness. However, self-compassion and forgiveness offer a different perspective that acknowledges our inherent humanity and allows us to embrace our imperfections with kindness.

As we embark on the path of healing, cultivating self-compassion becomes an essential step. It is about recognizing that our pain is not a reflection of personal failure but a natural response to our challenging circumstances. It is understanding that healing takes time, and it is okay to permit ourselves to heal at our own pace.

Through self-compassion and forgiveness, we create a safe and nurturing inner space to acknowledge our pain, honour our emotions, and offer ourselves the support we need. This means allowing ourselves to feel the depths of our sorrow, anger, or grief without judgment or resistance. It means embracing the truth that healing is not linear and that setbacks are a natural part of the journey.

Self-compassion and forgiveness also involve recognizing our shared humanity. We are not alone in our struggles. Others have experienced similar pain and have embarked on their paths of healing. By acknowledging our shared humanity, we foster a sense of connection and empathy, which can help alleviate the isolation and shame often accompany emotional hurts.

When we approach our healing journey with self-compassion and forgiveness, we create a solid foundation for letting go. It becomes easier to release the grip of past wounds because we no longer carry the weight of self-blame or the burden of harsh judgments. Instead, we offer ourselves the same understanding and forgiveness we would extend to others.

Practicing self-compassion and forgiveness can take many forms. It may involve gentle self-talk, acknowledging your pain and offering words of comfort and encouragement. It may entail engaging in soothing self-care practices that nourish your soul (mind, will and emotions), body, and spirit. It may also mean seeking support from trusted individuals who can hold space for your healing process with compassion and empathy.

Cultivating self-compassion and forgiveness is a sign of strength. It requires courage to embrace our vulnerabilities and treat ourselves with kindness in the face of pain. By cultivating self-compassion, we open the door to deep healing and transformation, allowing ourselves to let go of the past and step into a future filled with love, acceptance, and growth.

We need to embrace ourselves with kindness, tenderness, and understanding. Trust in our ability to heal and release the weight of past hurts. We are deserving of compassion and forgiveness, and by extending it to ourselves, we create the space for profound healing and the freedom to create a life filled with joy and self-discovery.

Understanding the impact of emotional hurts brings clarity to the weight these hurt carry in our lives. They shape our thoughts, emotions, and behaviours, impacting our self-esteem, relationships, and overall well-being. We can divert our thoughts on paper to avoid saying the wrong things out of frustration. So many of us carry regrets as we vent to our loved ones saying hurtful words we cannot take back. We can empty our thoughts and manipulate the mind

Imagine holding a pen in your hand, poised above a blank page. With each stroke of the pen, you create a safe and sacred space to express yourself fully, honestly, and without judgment. This act of journaling becomes an intimate conversation with yourself, a space where you can freely explore the depths of your emotions, thoughts, and experiences.

Journaling is a therapeutic tool that allows us to process and release emotional hurts. Through the act of writing, we give voice to our pain, bringing it out from the depths of our being and onto the pages before us. We give ourselves permission to express our anger, sadness, confusion, and any other emotions that may have been buried beneath the surface.

The act of putting pen to paper is a form of catharsis. As

we write, we engage our logical and emotional faculties, bridging the conscious and subconscious mind. We unravel the tangled threads of our thoughts and feelings, gaining clarity and insight into the impact of past hurts on our present lives.

Journaling allows us to explore the layers of our experiences. We can delve into the specific moments that caused us pain, reflecting on the circumstances, the people involved, and the emotions that arose. We can also explore the patterns that have emerged from these hurts, noticing recurring themes or triggers that still affect us today.

We may find ourselves unearthing buried memories, unexpressed emotions, and deep-seated beliefs as we write. This process can be both liberating and challenging. It requires courage to confront our pain head-on, but in doing so, we create an opportunity for healing and growth.

Through journaling, we release our emotions and gain valuable insights. We may uncover patterns of behaviour or recurring thoughts influenced by our past hurts. We may discover limiting beliefs that have prevented us from embracing our full potential. By shining a light on these insights, we open the door to transformation and empower ourselves to make conscious choices that align with our true desires.

Journaling is a deeply personal practice. There are no rules or right or wrong ways to do it. Allow yourself the freedom to write without judgment, letting your thoughts and emotions flow onto the pages. Write as often as you feel called to, whether daily, weekly, or whenever the need arises. The key is consistency and a commitment to creating a space for your innermost self to be heard.

Journaling for emotional release is a journey of self-discovery and healing. It is a process that unfolds over time, gradually unravelling the layers of pain and revealing the seeds of resilience and growth within us. As you embark on this practice, be gentle with yourself and celebrate the courage it takes to confront your hurts and begin the process of letting go.

We don't have to walk alone in our journey of healing and letting go. The weight of emotional hurts can sometimes feel overwhelming, but remember that there is a network of support waiting to uplift and guide you along the way. We must explore the importance of seeking support and how it can play a vital role in your healing process.

Imagine standing at the edge of a vast forest, unsure which path to take. The dense trees and tangled undergrowth seem insurmountable. But then, you notice a guiding light in the distance. The light of support leads you toward a more precise and hopeful future.

Support networks come in various forms, each offering a unique set of resources and understanding. They can include trusted friends, family members, support groups, therapists, or helplines. These individuals and communities provide a listening ear, empathy, and guidance as we navigate the complexities of healing.

In letting go of a hurt mind, there comes a pivotal moment when we must confront the impact these wounds have had on our self-identity. The stones in our backpacks weigh us emotionally and shape how we perceive ourselves and our self-worth. At this juncture, we embark on the powerful task of redefining our self-identity, rebuilding a sense of self-worth, and forging a new path forward.

When a hurt mind have been deeply ingrained, it's common to internalize the negative messages they carry. You may find yourself believing that you are unworthy, unlovable, or fundamentally flawed. The wounds may have created a distorted lens through which you view yourself, casting a shadow of doubt and self-criticism on your every thought and action.

We are not defined by the pain we've experienced. We are not limited by our mistakes or hurtful words that have been hurled at us. We have within us a wellspring of resilience, strength, and untapped potential that can lead to a profound transformation of our self-identity.

The process of redefining self-identity begins with self-compassion and self-acceptance. It requires acknowledging that the hurtful experiences we've endured do not diminish our worth as human beings. It involves challenging negative beliefs and replacing them with affirming and empowering thoughts about us.

We are not broken. We are a survivor. We have weathered storms and emerged stronger. Embrace the journey of self-discovery and self-compassion, and you will begin to uncover the beautiful qualities and unique strengths that emotional hurts have overshadowed.

As we redefine our self-identity, engaging in reflective practices, including journaling, meditation, or therapy, can be helpful. These tools allow us to explore our values, passions, and strengths. They allow us to reconnect with the authentic essence of who we are, separate from the wounds and the narratives that have defined us in the past.

Take small, intentional steps towards self-care and self-nurturing. Engage in activities that bring you joy and ignite your passions. Cultivate self-compassion by speaking kindly to yourself and acknowledging your progress along this transformative journey. Healing is not a linear process; there will be ups and downs. Be patient and gentle with yourself as you navigate the twists and turns.

In time, you will begin to rebuild a sense of self-worth and authentic identity aligned with your truest self. You will embrace your strengths and imperfections, celebrating the unique individual that you are. Through this redefinition, you will create a solid foundation from which to move forward, guided by your newfound sense of self and purpose.

Let us cast off the labels and beliefs that no longer serve

us and step into the light of our inherent worthiness. Remember that you deserve love, joy, and a fulfilling life. Embrace the process of redefining your self-identity and allow yourself to soar to new heights of self-discovery, empowerment, and happiness.

For some, releasing emotional hurts may mean practicing expressive arts therapy. When words alone cannot capture the depth of our emotions or adequately express our pain, creative outlets provide an alternative avenue for release and transformation.

Expressive arts therapy encompasses a variety of artistic mediums, including visual arts, music, dance, writing, and drama. It invites us to step beyond the constraints of language and tap into the vast realm of our imagination and intuition. Through creative expression, we can explore the depths of our emotional pain, give it form and substance, and ultimately release it from the depths of our being.

Imagine a blank canvas before you, waiting patiently for your brush to dance across its surface. Something magical happens as you dip the brush into vibrant paint and allow it to glide, swirl, and collide with the canvas. The colours, lines, and textures take shape, becoming a visual representation of your emotions, thoughts, and experiences. With each stroke, you imbue a part of yourself onto the canvas, externalizing the internal landscape of your emotional pain.

Similarly, music can become a conduit for emotional

expression. Whether through playing an instrument, singing, or even just listening to carefully selected songs, music has the power to tap into the depths of our souls. The melodies, harmonies, and rhythms can mirror the ebb and flow of our emotions, allowing us to release pain, find solace, and ultimately experience catharsis.

Dance, too, becomes a language of the body, a non-verbal expression of our innermost feelings. As we allow our bodies to move freely, guided by music and emotions, we can release pent-up tension, unspoken sorrows, and untold stories. Through dance, we reconnect with the innate wisdom of our bodies and unlock the ability to move through our pain with grace and fluidity.

Writing, whether in the form of journaling, poetry, or storytelling, grants us the power to weave words into healing tapestries. As we put pen to paper, we give voice to our emotions, allowing them to flow freely without judgment or limitation. We can explore our pain, reflect on our experiences, and discover new insights and perspectives that lead us toward healing and understanding.

The transformative potential of drama and theatre can impact letting go of ourselves, bringing healing to emotional wounds. Through acting, improvisation, or role-playing, we can step into the shoes of different characters and explore their narratives. Doing so gives us a fresh perspective on our lives and emotional pain. We can experiment with alternative endings, rewrite our stories, and discover the strength and resilience within ourselves.

Expressive arts therapy is not about creating masterpieces or achieving perfection. It is about providing a safe and non-judgmental space to express and release the emotional pain that words alone may struggle to convey. It offers a means of communication that transcends the limitations of language, allowing us to connect deeply with ourselves and others.

As we explore creative outlets for emotional release, remember that the process is deeply personal. There are no right or wrong ways to engage in expressive arts therapy. What matters most is your willingness to explore, experiment, and permit yourself to let go. Embrace the freedom to express yourself authentically and discover the healing potential of these artistic expressions.

Let us tap into the limitless reservoir of our creativity and allow it to guide us toward healing and wholeness. Through expressive arts therapy, we can unlock the doors to our emotions and find solace, understanding, and transformation.

In exploring the impact of a hurt mind, we must understand the weight it carries and how they shape our lives. We have acknowledged the burden of carrying these hurts and have begun to uncover the power within us to heal and let go. We need to tap into the strength of resiliency if we want to move on with our lives.

Resilience is the ability to bounce back from adversity and rise above the challenges that life throws us. It is not about denying or ignoring the pain of past hurts; instead, it is about acknowledging the pain and choosing not to let it define us. It is about recognizing that we have the strength within us to heal, grow, and create a future that is not overshadowed by our past.

Embracing a mindset of resilience begins with reframing our perspective. Instead of viewing past hurts as permanent scars, we can view them as stepping stones that have shaped us into the resilient individuals we are today. Each hurt we have endured has taught us valuable lessons about ourselves, others, and the world. It has equipped us with wisdom, compassion, and the strength to overcome future challenges.

Resilience involves cultivating self-compassion. We must extend kindness and understanding to ourselves as we navigate the healing process. It is essential to remember that healing takes time and that setbacks may occur. We must offer ourselves the same love and support we would give to friends or loved ones, allowing ourselves space to grieve, heal, and grow at our own pace.

As we become resilient, we must surround ourselves with a supportive network of individuals who uplift and encourage us, as discussed earlier in this chapter. Trusted friends, family members, or support groups can provide invaluable emotional support, guidance, and validation. Their presence reminds us that we are not alone in our journey and that there are others who have walked a similar path of healing and growth.

Moreover, embracing resilience means embracing growth. It is through the process of healing that we unearth our true potential and discover new strengths within ourselves. By acknowledging and processing our past hurts, we can uncover patterns and behaviours that no longer serve us and actively work towards positive change. We can choose to break free from self-limiting beliefs and cultivate new empowering narratives that propel us forward.

Moving forward with resilience does not mean the road ahead will be without challenges. It means we have the inner fortitude to face those challenges head-on, armed with the wisdom and strength gained from our healing journey. Resilience enables us to adapt, learn, and grow from our experiences, transforming our pain into purpose and our wounds into wisdom.

In conclusion, we embarked on a transformative journey to understand and heal from our a hurt mind. We delved deep into the impact of past wounds on our present well-being, and we bravely faced hidden resentments that had been holding us back. Along the way, we discovered the immense power of forgiveness as a path to healing, learning that it is not about condoning the actions of others but about liberating ourselves from the shackles of pain.

OUR MIND

Our mind is a complex and dynamic system that encompasses the workings of the brain, consciousness, thoughts, emotions, and perceptions. It is the source of a person's thoughts, feelings, memories, and experiences. The mind is responsible for our ability to perceive and interpret information from the world around us, form memories and store them, think, make decisions, and experience emotions. It is often described as being the seat of a person's consciousness and self-awareness. The mind is an intangible and abstract concept, but it is widely recognized as having a significant impact on our overall well-being and quality of life.

The first and biggest teacher to our mind is our environment which is a mixture of good and bad happenings.

Good events and positive experiences can have a profound impact on our minds and overall well-being. When we experience positive emotions, our brain releases neurotransmitters like dopamine and serotonin, which can boost our mood and feelings of happiness, reduce stress and anxiety, and improve our overall mental well-being. For example, getting a promotion at work, reuniting with a long-lost friend, or accomplishing a personal goal can all bring joy and a sense of fulfillment, making us feel good both mentally and emotionally.

Additionally, positive experiences can also enhance our self-esteem and increase our sense of purpose, helping to create a more positive outlook on life. These positive effects can last for a while and even help to improve our mood and outlook on life in general. Good life happenings create a positive and supportive internal and external environment, and promote overall mental and emotional health, allowing us to live happier, more fulfilling lives.

However, as we know, life is not a bed of roses; it has its own thorns too. Our life is filled with blessings and condemnations that are continuously happening to us. Good happenings and misfortunate events go hand in hand, and all these life adventures have a direct impact on our minds. As we know, our mind is more negatively biased so, it is obvious that our mind is more prone to damage by life incidents that are against our wills. Bad events, such as accidents, assaults, or natural disasters, can leave a real impact on a person's mind and emotions. When something traumatic happens, it can be tough to shake the feelings and thoughts that come with it. For example, after a bad event, we might feel overwhelmed by feelings of fear, anger, or sadness. We may find it difficult to have a sound sleep, eat properly, or enjoy things that used to bring us happiness. Sometimes, memories of the event can pop up unexpectedly, causing flashbacks or nightmares. This can all make it tough to feel like yourself again. On top of these emotional struggles, we might also experience physical symptoms, like headaches, stomach problems, or a racing heart. All of these symptoms can add up to make someone feel pretty rough and with a wounded mind.

We all have moments when our minds aren't feeling their best. But what sets a healthy mind apart from a wounded one? Well, a healthy mind is one that is able to handle the ups and downs of life without getting too frazzled or upset. With a sound mind, we can think clearly, make good decisions, and have positive relationships with the people around us. In simple terms, you can say that a healthy mind is one that is feeling good - that's all! Basically, a healthy mind is like a well-oiled machine – everything is working together smoothly. And, just like our body, it takes effort and cares to keep our mind healthy. So, if we are feeling good and handling life with ease, then there are strong chances that we have a pretty healthy mind.

On the flip side, a wounded mind has been through some tough stuff – whether it's a traumatic event, abuse or neglect, substance abuse, chronic stress, or grief and loss. These experiences can leave a lasting impact and cause symptoms like anxiety, depression, fear, guilt, and shame. Do you know what really wounds our minds? There are a lot of things, but some of the most common include traumatic events like natural disasters or violence, being mistreated or neglected as a child, substance abuse, constant stress, losing someone close to you, or dealing with chronic physical health problems. It is worth remembering that a wounded mind doesn't mean we are weak or hopeless. In fact, it takes a lot of strength to keep going despite these struggles.

Likewise, everyone is different and their experiences with mental health can be unique but with the right support and treatment, many people are able to recover and have a healthy mind again.

Psychological injuries that result from negative experiences such as trauma, rejection, loss, or abuse. They can affect our emotions, thoughts, and behaviour, and can be long-lasting if left unaddressed. These wounds are often hidden from others and may be hard to recognize or admit to ourselves. A hurt mind can manifest in a variety of ways. They can cause us to feel anxious, depressed, angry, or hopeless. They can also lead to self-destructive behaviors such as substance abuse, overeating, or self-harm. Emotional wounds can be triggered by events or situations that remind us of the original trauma, leading to a cascade of negative emotions and thoughts.

Lily was a young woman who had grown up in a dysfunctional family. Her parents had a lot of issues, and they frequently fought, leaving Lily feeling anxious and insecure. As a result, she developed a deep fear of abandonment and struggled with trust issues in her relationships. One day, Lily fell in love with a man named Alex, and they started dating. However, Alex had a busy job and often had to work late, which triggered Lily's fear of abandonment. She would worry that he was cheating on her or that he didn't really love her, even though he reassured her that he did.

As time went on, Lily's insecurities started to impact their relationship. She would become jealous and possessive, accusing Jake of things he hadn't done. Eventually, Alex couldn't take it anymore and ended the relationship, leaving Lily feeling devastated and alone. Even though Lily tried to move on, the emotional wounds from her childhood and the breakup with Jake continued to impact her. She found herself struggling with depression and anxiety and had trouble trusting anyone else. It wasn't until Lily sought the help of a therapist that she was able to start healing her emotional wounds. Through therapy, she was able to understand how her past experiences had shaped her behavior and beliefs and learn new coping mechanisms to manage her anxiety and insecurity.

With time, Lily started to feel more confident and began to trust herself and others again. She even started dating someone new, and although it wasn't always easy, she was able to build a healthy relationship based on trust and mutual respect.

Through her journey of healing, Lily learned that emotional wounds can have a significant impact on our lives, but that with the right support and self-care, it is possible to move forward and live a fulfilling life. So, if you are facing a similar situation then remember, you are not alone on this journey, and with support and love, everything will be alright at the end – just trust the process!

From Lily's story, it is clear that a hurt mind can have a significant impact on our mental health and brain function. They can affect our thoughts, emotions, and behavior, and can lead to a range of mental health issues such as anxiety, depression, post-traumatic stress disorder (PTSD), and addiction. Above all, a hurt mind can affect our ability to form healthy relationships. If we have experienced rejection or abandonment, we may have difficulty trusting others and forming close connections. This can lead to feelings of isolation and loneliness, which can further exacerbate mental health issues. These wounds even lead to changes in brain function and structure. Studies have shown that prolonged stress, such as that caused by trauma, can result in changes in the brain's structure, function, and chemistry. This can lead to a range of issues, such as difficulty regulating emotions, memory problems, and difficulty concentrating.

Ultimately, healing from hurts is a journey, and it's important to approach it with a sense of curiosity and openness. By acknowledging and addressing emotional wounds, individuals can learn to live more fully in the present moment and move forward with a greater sense of resilience and self-awareness. Hurts can impact each person differently, and there's no right or wrong way to feel after experiencing trauma or distressing events. However, if the wounds are left unaddressed, they can lead to a messed up brain and make it difficult for the person to move forward in their life.

MENTAL TOUGHNESS

Developing Mental Toughness explores various strategies and techniques to help you cultivate and strengthen your mental resilience. By embracing these practices, you will be well-equipped to navigate life's challenges and obstacles with a positive mindset and unwavering determination.

Mental toughness is not an innate quality reserved for a select few; instead, it is a skill that can be developed and honed over time. It enables you to face adversity head-on, bounce back from setbacks, and flourish in the face of change. By focusing on the power of your mind, you can unlock the potential within you to overcome obstacles and thrive in all areas of your life.

This chapter will delve into the fundamental aspects of developing mental toughness. You will discover the importance of recognizing and challenging negative self-talk and techniques to build resilience when faced with adversity. We will explore the transformative effects of embracing change and cultivating adaptability, along with the role of a growth mindset in fostering mental toughness.

Moreover, we will discuss the significance of setting realistic goals, overcoming obstacles, and harnessing the power of perseverance. You will also learn valuable strategies for managing stress and anxiety effectively, building confidence, and enhancing self-efficacy. Additionally, we will explore methods to improve focus and concentration and the transformative impact of mindfulness and meditation on mental toughness.

To better understand mental toughness, we need to explore the mental fortitude that will empower us to thrive in any situation. It will equip us with the tools and knowledge necessary to cultivate a positive and resilient mindset. It will enable us to face challenges head-on and persevere even when the going gets tough.

Remember, developing mental toughness is a continuous process. It requires dedication, practice, and a commitment to personal growth. As we embark on mental toughness, be open to new perspectives and willing to embrace change. With each step you take, you will discover the remarkable strength within you, empowering you to conquer obstacles, achieve your goals, and live a fulfilling life.

One of the critical foundations of mental toughness lies in recognizing and challenging negative self-talk. Our minds have an incredible power to shape our reality, and how we talk to ourselves internally can significantly influence our emotions, behaviours, and overall well-being. We can rewire our brains to transform negative self-talk into positive and empowering affirmations.

Negative self-talk often manifests as self-criticism, doubt, and limiting beliefs that hold us back from reaching our full potential. It is a roadblock to our growth and can significantly impact our confidence and self-esteem. However, by consciously recognizing these negative thought patterns, we can begin the process of rewiring our brains for positive change.

By becoming aware of our negative self-talk, we can challenge and replace these destructive thoughts with more positive and supportive ones. This process involves reframing our perspective and cultivating self-compassion. Instead of criticizing ourselves for perceived shortcomings or failures, we can choose to respond with kindness and understanding.

According to a study by Mosewich et al. (2018), cognitive restructuring exercises can effectively identify negative patterns and replace them with affirmations that reinforce strengths, capabilities, and self-worth. These exercises empower individuals to develop a more optimistic and resilient mindset, enabling them to face challenges confidently and continuously.

Through consistent practice and reinforcement of positive messages, it is possible to rewire the brain to believe in one's abilities and potential. These empowering statements become integral to daily life, fostering a solid foundation of self-belief and resilience.

It is essential to approach the journey of rewiring the brain with patience and self-acceptance, as developing mental toughness is gradual. By committing to challenging negative self-talk and embracing positive affirmations, individuals take a significant step towards empowering themselves and creating a more fulfilling life.

Recognizing and challenging negative self-talk unlocks the immense potential within individuals and cultivates a mindset that can overcome any obstacle. We can build a solid foundation of self-belief, resilience, and mental toughness, empowering individuals to thrive in all aspects of life.

Change is an inevitable part of life, and developing mental toughness involves embracing it with a positive and open mindset. We must tap into the transformative power of embracing change and cultivating adaptability and how these qualities can contribute to your mental toughness.

Change provides us with opportunities for growth, self-discovery, and personal development. We open ourselves to new possibilities, experiences, and perspectives by embracing change. Rather than fearing or resisting change, we can choose to see it as a catalyst for progress and transformation.

One of the critical aspects of developing mental toughness is recognizing that change is often accompanied by uncertainty and the unknown. It requires a willingness to step outside our comfort zone and explore uncharted territories. Doing so broadens our horizons and expands our capabilities, fostering personal growth and resilience.

Adaptability goes hand in hand with embracing change. It is the ability to adjust and thrive in different situations, even when circumstances constantly evolve. A mentally tough individual possesses the flexibility and resilience to adapt their mindset, strategies, and actions to meet the demands of a changing environment.

When we cultivate adaptability, we develop a remarkable ability to navigate challenges and setbacks effectively. Instead of becoming overwhelmed or discouraged by unexpected circumstances, we see them as opportunities to learn, evolve, and find creative solutions. This mindset allows us to maintain control and optimism, even when faced with adversity.

Moreover, embracing change and cultivating adaptability can increase self-confidence and self-belief. As we navigate new experiences and overcome obstacles, we develop a deep-rooted trust in our ability to handle whatever comes our way. This self-assurance becomes a solid foundation for our mental toughness, enabling us to face future challenges with unwavering resolve.

In a world constantly evolving and presenting new challenges, embracing change and cultivating adaptability is a valuable asset. It allows us to thrive in dynamic environments, seize opportunities, and stay ahead of the curve. By fostering these qualities, we position ourselves for success and personal fulfilment.

Embracing change and cultivating adaptability is a process that requires patience and self-reflection. Embrace the unknown with a positive attitude, seek growth opportunities, and trust your ability to adapt and thrive. By doing so, you will develop the mental toughness necessary to navigate life's ever-changing landscape and emerge stronger, wiser, and more resilient.

In the realm of mental toughness, few attributes are as transformative as a growth mindset. A growth mindset is a powerful belief that our abilities and intelligence can be developed and improved through dedication, effort, and a willingness to learn. It is the belief that challenges are growth opportunities, and setbacks are merely stepping stones on the path to success. By cultivating a growth mindset, we open ourselves to a world of possibilities and unleash our true potential.

Embracing a growth mindset is an invitation to view failures not as permanent limitations but as valuable lessons and opportunities for growth. Instead of being discouraged by setbacks, those with a growth mindset approach them with curiosity and resilience. They see obstacles as puzzles to solve and setbacks as temporary roadblocks on the journey toward their goals. They see obstacles as opportunities and failures as fertilizers for their future.

One of the most remarkable aspects of a growth mindset is its ability to reshape how we perceive our abilities and potential. With a growth mindset, we understand that intelligence and talents are not fixed traits but qualities that can be developed over time. This realization liberates us from the constraints of self-imposed limitations and allows us to embrace continuous learning and improvement.

By cultivating a growth mindset, we become more open to taking on challenges outside our comfort zone. We must recognize that stepping into the unknown is an opportunity for personal and professional growth. This willingness to push boundaries and embrace new experiences fosters resilience and adaptability, crucial qualities for navigating life's ever-changing landscape.

Moreover, a growth mindset encourages a positive attitude toward effort and perseverance. Instead of viewing hard work as a burden, individuals with a growth mindset see it as essential to growth and success. They understand that with consistent effort and deliberate practice, they can achieve mastery in any area they choose.

Furthermore, a growth mindset nurtures a love for

learning. It encourages a thirst for knowledge, the exploration of new ideas, and a willingness to seek feedback and constructive criticism. This continuous pursuit of education fuels personal and professional growth, propelling individuals toward their goals with unwavering determination.

Cultivating a growth mindset can be developed and strengthened over time. Practice self-compassion and embrace a positive and patient attitude toward your growth. Celebrate your progress and the small victories along the way, for they are stepping stones toward your larger aspirations.

Unlock your true potential, embrace challenges as opportunities for growth, and set out on a path of continuous learning and self-improvement. With a growth mindset as our guiding light, there are no limits to what we can achieve.

Setting realistic goals is a vital component of developing mental toughness. It involves envisioning our desired outcomes and creating a roadmap to achieve them. Setting clear, achievable goals lays the foundation for success and creates a positive mindset that propels us forward.

When setting our goals, it's crucial to balance ambition and realism. While it's important to challenge ourselves, setting overly ambitious goals can lead to frustration and demotivation if they are consistently out of reach. Setting realistic goals creates a sense of achievement and momentum, fuelling our motivation and fostering a positive outlook.

In achieving our goals, we will inevitably encounter

obstacles along the way. These obstacles may come in various forms, such as unexpected setbacks, self-doubt, or external challenges. However, we can overcome these obstacles by cultivating mental toughness and continue moving forward toward our aspirations.

Obstacles are not roadblocks; they are opportunities for growth and learning. With a positive mindset and unwavering determination, we can reframe obstacles as stepping stones to success. Each challenge we encounter serves as a chance to develop resilience, problem-solving skills, and adaptability.

When faced with obstacles, it's essential to approach them with a solution-oriented mindset. Instead of dwelling on the problem, focus on identifying potential solutions and taking proactive steps to overcome them. Embrace the philosophy that every setback is a valuable learning experience, providing insights and knowledge to benefit us in the long run.

Remember, the path to success is rarely a straight line. There will be detours, setbacks, and unexpected hurdles. However, with a positive mindset, realistic goals, and the mental toughness to overcome obstacles, we have the power to navigate these challenges and emerge more robust than ever.

Celebrate your progress along the way, and face obstacles head-on with unwavering determination. Through this journey, we will not only achieve our desired outcomes but also cultivate resilience, inner strength, and an unyielding belief in our ability to overcome any challenge that comes our way.

Perseverance, the unwavering determination to keep going despite challenges and setbacks, is a remarkable quality that can propel us toward success and personal growth. There is tremendous power that perseverance holds and how it can contribute to the development of mental toughness in the most positive and uplifting way.

When faced with obstacles and difficulties, it is natural to feel discouraged or tempted to give up. However, by embracing the power of perseverance, we can transform these moments into opportunities for growth and achievement. Through determination, we learn to rise above our circumstances, push our limits, and discover the strength and resilience that lie within us.

One of the critical aspects of developing mental toughness through perseverance is maintaining a positive attitude in the face of adversity. Challenges may seem daunting at first, but cultivating a mindset focused on finding solutions and learning from setbacks can maintain an optimistic outlook even in the toughest of times. With each challenge overcome, our confidence grows, and we become better equipped to face future hurdles.

Perseverance allows us to develop resilience. As discussed earlier, it teaches us that failure is not the end but rather an opportunity to learn and improve. By viewing setbacks as stepping stones toward success, we can embrace a growth mindset and continually evolve as an individual.

Moreover, the power of perseverance lies in its ability to keep us motivated and driven toward our goals. It instils in us a sense of determination and commitment to see things through, even when faced with obstacles that may seem insurmountable. We increase our chances of achieving desired results by maintaining a steadfast focus on our objectives and refusing to give up.

Perseverance is not a solitary pursuit; it can also be bolstered by seeking support from others. Surrounding ourselves with a strong support network of like-minded individuals who encourage and inspire us can significantly enhance our ability to persevere. Sharing our challenges and triumphs with others fosters a sense of camaraderie and provides valuable insights and encouragement along the way.

As we harness the power of perseverance, remember that it is a skill that can be cultivated and strengthened over time. Each small step we take, each setback we overcome, and each achievement we celebrate will contribute to our growth and resilience. Embrace perseverance as a lifelong companion, and we will find that it holds the key to unlocking our full potential and achieving remarkable success.

In today's fast-paced world, stress and anxiety have become increasingly prevalent. However, we view these challenges as opportunities for growth and self-improvement within the realm of developing mental toughness. We can manage stress and anxiety effectively, empowering ourselves to navigate life's pressures with grace and resilience.

It is important to recognize that stress and anxiety are natural responses to the demands and uncertainties of everyday life. They are signals from our bodies and minds, indicating the need for attention and care. Adopting a positive perspective can transform these experiences into catalysts for personal growth, developing the mental toughness needed to thrive in any situation.

One powerful approach to managing stress and anxiety is through the cultivation of healthy coping mechanisms. These mechanisms may include engaging in physical exercise, practicing relaxation techniques, or participating in activities that bring us joy and a sense of calm. By incorporating these strategies into our daily routine, we can create a foundation of resilience, allowing ourselves to face stressors with a positive mindset.

Developing practical stress management skills also involves adopting a proactive approach to problem-solving. By identifying the root causes of stress and anxiety, we can implement practical solutions and positively change our lives. This proactive mindset not only alleviates immediate stress but also equips us with the ability to anticipate and mitigate future challenges.

Nurturing our physical, emotional, and mental well-being is crucial for developing mental toughness. Engaging in activities that bring us joy, practicing mindfulness, and prioritizing restful sleep are all integral parts of a self-care routine that can fortify our resilience.

Ultimately, managing stress and anxiety effectively empowers us to control our thoughts, emotions, and responses. Adopting a positive mindset and embracing these strategies can transform stress and anxiety into stepping stones toward personal growth and increased mental toughness. With each challenge we overcome, we will emerge more assertive, resilient, and better equipped to navigate life's complexities.

With dedication, practice, and the tools available, we can be empowered to face stress and anxiety head-on, transforming them into catalysts for personal growth and unwavering mental toughness.

Confidence and self-efficacy are potent attributes that contribute to mental toughness. When we possess a strong sense of confidence, we believe in our abilities and have faith in our capacity to succeed. Self-efficacy, conversely, is the belief in our capability to accomplish specific tasks or goals. Together, they form a dynamic duo that empowers us to overcome challenges and seize opportunities with a positive outlook.

There are various strategies and techniques to help build and bolster our confidence and self-efficacy. By embracing these practices, we will cultivate an unshakable belief in ourselves, enabling us to tackle obstacles and achieve our aspirations with resilience and determination.

One of the critical foundations for building confidence and self-efficacy is recognizing and celebrating our strengths and accomplishments. We can believe in our capabilities by acknowledging our unique abilities and previous successes. Remember, no matter how small, each achievement is a stepping stone towards more remarkable accomplishments. We must embrace these triumph moments and let them fuel our confidence to take on new challenges.

Another vital aspect of building confidence and self-efficacy is challenging self-doubt and negative self-talk. Replace self-defeating thoughts with positive affirmations and constructive self-talk. We must encourage ourselves, remind ourselves of past successes, and focus on our potential for growth. We create a supportive mental environment that fosters confidence and self-belief by cultivating a positive internal dialogue.

Additionally, seeking out new experiences and pushing ourselves beyond our comfort zone can be instrumental in building confidence and self-efficacy. Embrace opportunities that allow us to learn and grow, even if they initially seem daunting. Each new experience provides a chance to prove that we are capable of more than we may have thought originally. With each successful encounter, our confidence will naturally flourish, and our self-efficacy will strengthen.

We must practice self-care and engage in activities that

nourish our minds, bodies, and spirits. Taking care of ourselves physically and emotionally contributes to a positive self-image and an enhanced sense of self-worth. Engage in activities that bring us happiness, practice self-compassion, and embrace self-acceptance. The more we prioritize self-care, our confidence and self-efficacy will flourish.

Building confidence and self-efficacy is an ongoing journey requiring patience and perseverance. As we incorporate these strategies into our lives, we will witness a remarkable transformation in how we perceive ourselves and our abilities. With a solid foundation of confidence and self-efficacy, we will approach challenges with resilience, embrace new opportunities, and ultimately achieve our goals with unwavering determination.

In today's fast-paced and increasingly distracted world, focusing and concentrating has become precious skill. Fortunately, it is a skill that can be cultivated and enhanced through dedicated practice and a positive mindset. Some strategies and techniques can help us sharpen our focus and concentration, enabling us to achieve greater productivity and success.

When we enhance our focus and concentration, we unlock a world of possibilities. Imagine fully immersing ourselves in a task, free from distractions and interruptions. By developing this skill, we can tap into a state of flow where time seems to slip away and our productivity soars. Whether studying for an important exam, working on a challenging project, or engaging in any activity that requires our undivided attention, the ability to concentrate profoundly is a game-changer.

One powerful method to enhance focus and concentration is to create an optimal environment. Designate a specific workspace that is free from clutter and distractions. Minimize external noise and create a comfortable atmosphere that allows our minds to engage with the task at hand fully. By creating a dedicated space for focused work, we signal to our minds that it is time to concentrate and eliminate potential sources of interruption.

Another effective strategy is to manage our time effectively. Break our tasks into smaller, manageable chunks and allocate specific time blocks for focused work. Use techniques like the Pomodoro Technique, where we work in concentrated bursts of time followed by short breaks. This helps maintain our focus and prevents burnout and mental fatigue. With consistent practice, we will find that our ability to concentrate for extended periods improves, and our productivity skyrockets.

In addition to external factors, cultivating a positive mindset is vital for enhancing focus and concentration. Develop a sense of curiosity and interest in the task at hand. Approach it with enthusiasm and a genuine desire to immerse yourself in the subject matter. By cultivating a positive attitude, we create an internal motivation that fuels our focus and concentration, making the experience more enjoyable and rewarding.

Remember, developing enhanced focus and concentration is a gradual process that requires patience and persistence. Celebrate small victories along the way and acknowledge the progress we make, no matter how small. With each dedicated effort, we are building the foundation for a focused and concentrated mind to empower us to excel in all areas of our lives. By honing this skill, we set ourselves up for success and unlock our full potential. We must unleash our laser-like focus and achieve remarkable results in all our endeavours.

One powerful and transformative tool at our disposal is the practice of mindfulness and meditation. By incorporating these practices into our daily lives, we can cultivate a positive and resilient mindset, enhance our emotional well-being, and strengthen our ability to face challenges with unwavering resolve.

Mindfulness is the art of being fully present and engaged in the present moment without judgment or attachment. It involves redirecting our attention away from past or future distractions and immersing ourselves in the richness of the current experience. Through mindfulness, we develop an acute awareness of our thoughts, emotions, and physical sensations, enabling us to respond to them consciously rather than being swept away.

Meditation, on the other hand, is a specific practice that encompasses various techniques to quiet the mind, cultivate inner peace, and foster self-awareness. It often involves focusing our attention on a particular object, such as our breath or a mantra, to anchor our thoughts and promote a state of calmness and clarity.

When it comes to mental toughness, mindfulness and meditation offer numerous benefits. Firstly, they help us develop inner strength and resilience by cultivating a deeper understanding of our thoughts and emotions. Regular practice makes us more adept at recognizing and managing negative thoughts and self-doubt, allowing us to maintain a positive and focused mindset even in challenging situations.

Furthermore, mindfulness and meditation provide valuable tools for managing stress and anxiety effectively. By bringing our attention to the present moment, we can detach ourselves from worries about the past or future, reducing the impact of stressors on our mental well-being. These practices promote relaxation and calmness, enabling us to approach difficult situations clearly and composedly.

In addition, mindfulness and meditation enhance our ability to concentrate and maintain focus. Cultivating a disciplined mind becomes crucial for mental toughness in a world filled with distractions. By training ourselves to anchor our attention to the present moment through these practices, we can enhance our concentration, heighten our awareness, and stay resilient despite distractions and obstacles.

Moreover, mindfulness and meditation foster self-compassion and self-acceptance. They invite us to observe our thoughts and emotions with curiosity and kindness, without judgment or criticism. This practice of self-compassion enables us to develop a healthy relationship with ourselves, enhancing our self-esteem and self-efficacy.

Practicing mindfulness and meditation for mental toughness is a journey of self-discovery and self-mastery. It empowers us to tap into our inner resilience and wisdom, allowing us to respond to life's challenges with grace and grit. By incorporating these practices into our daily lives, we embark on a path of personal growth, developing the mental strength and clarity needed to overcome obstacles and thrive in all areas of our lives.

Dedicate time each day to stillness and self-reflection. Embrace the present moment with an open heart and a curious mind. As we embark on this transformative practice, we will unlock our profound potential and discover a newfound resilience that will guide us toward a life of strength, purpose, and fulfilment.

In conclusion, we have explored various strategies and techniques to cultivate a positive and resilient mindset. By embracing these practices, we have equipped ourselves with the tools to face adversity, overcome challenges, and thrive in all aspects of life.

We began by recognizing the power of challenging negative self-talk and building resilience through adversity. We discovered the transformative effects of embracing change and cultivating adaptability, along with the crucial role of a growth mindset in fostering mental toughness. Setting realistic goals and overcoming obstacles became a cornerstone of our journey, as did harnessing the power of perseverance.

We also delved into managing stress and anxiety effectively, building confidence and self-efficacy, and enhancing focus and concentration. Each of these aspects contributes to our overall mental toughness and empowers us to navigate life's ups and downs with grace and strength.

Lastly, we explored the profound impact of practicing mindfulness and meditation. By incorporating these practices into our daily lives, we discovered the ability to cultivate a calm and resilient mindset, manage stress, enhance self-awareness, and develop a compassionate relationship with ourselves.

Remember, developing mental toughness is a continuous process. It requires dedication, practice, and a commitment to personal growth. As we move forward, apply the knowledge and insights gained from this chapter in our daily lives. Let's embrace the challenges that come our way as opportunities for growth and learning. Let's celebrate our progress, no matter how small, and be patient with ourselves during setbacks.

Developing mental toughness is not about achieving perfection or never experiencing difficulties. It's about building the resilience and inner strength needed to overcome obstacles, bounce back from setbacks, and thrive amidst the uncertainties of life. It's about developing a mindset that sees challenges as stepping stones to growth and transformation. It's about rewiring our brains.

Let's carry the wisdom and practices gained. Let's embrace the power of our minds, trust in our abilities, and believe in our capacity to face any challenge that comes our way. With mental toughness, we possess the inner strength to persevere, the resilience to bounce back, and the unwavering determination to achieve our goals and live a fulfilling life. We should have confidence, resilience, and a renewed sense of purpose. We can embrace mental toughness, knowing that we have the strength within us to overcome anything that comes our way.

CONCLUSION

Reflecting on the journey through the realms of the Three Minds, we covered several related topics that can help us understand ourselves and others. This has been an eye-opening experience filled with personal growth, heartache, and profound understanding. This journey wasn't just about becoming mentally tough; it was about connecting deeply with myself and others, transforming my pain into strength, and discovering the power of collective empathy.

Looking back at my journey through the Three Minds—mastering the mind, understanding a hurt mind, and connecting with "our minds"—feels like flipping through the pages of a deeply personal and transformative story. This path has been more than just about building mental toughness; it's been a voyage of self-discovery, healing, and connecting with the collective strength of our shared experiences.

When I started this journey, I believed that mastering the mind was all about having absolute control over my thoughts and emotions. I imagined it as conquering a mountain, standing tall and unshakable. But as I walked this path, I realized it was less about control and more about understanding. There were moments when I felt on top of my game, where everything seemed to click into place. But there were also times when doubt and fear clouded my thoughts. It was during these low points that I learned the true meaning of mastery—not in being invincible, but in acknowledging my vulnerabilities and navigating through them with courage and grace. It felt like learning to dance with my thoughts, finding a rhythm that allowed me to move through life's challenges with a newfound sense of balance and confidence.

Confronting my hurt mind was like opening a box of old, forgotten letters, each one bringing back memories that were both painful and healing. It meant facing the shadows of my past, the wounds that had shaped who I am today. Some days, the weight of these memories felt overwhelming, like a heavy rain that just wouldn't stop. But as I allowed myself to sit with these feelings, to truly feel the sadness, the anger, and the regret, I began to heal. I learned that pain is not something to be feared or avoided, but a part of my story that adds depth and resilience to my character. It was through embracing my hurt mind that I found strength in my scars, understanding that each one tells a story of survival and growth. This process wasn't easy, but it was incredibly freeing, like shedding an old, heavy coat and stepping into the warmth of the sun.

The concept of "our minds" was a revelation to me, teaching me the importance of connection and shared humanity. I discovered that we are all part of a larger tapestry, each thread representing a unique story and experience. By opening up to others and allowing them to see my true self, I found a deep sense of belonging and understanding. There were countless moments of connection, where a shared glance or a simple conversation reminded me that I am not alone in my struggles or my joys. It was through these connections that I realized the power of community, the strength that comes from knowing that we are all in this together. This understanding has helped me see that mental toughness is not just about personal resilience, but also about drawing strength from the collective, from "our minds" working in harmony.

As I reflect on this journey, I see how each aspect of the Three Minds has contributed to my growth and development. Mastering my mind has given me clarity and purpose; understanding my hurt mind has provided healing and strength; and connecting with "our minds" has brought me a sense of belonging and collective resilience. This journey has taught me that mental toughness is not a static goal but a dynamic process, one that involves continuous learning, healing, and connecting with others.

My experience with the Three Minds has been deeply personal and transformative, a journey that has led me to a greater understanding of myself and my place in the world. It has shown me that true strength comes from embracing all parts of myself—the highs and the lows, the joys and the pains—and from finding connection and support in the shared human experience. As I move forward, I carry these lessons with me, ready to face whatever challenges come my way with a heart full of courage, a mind open to growth, and a spirit deeply connected to the collective strength of our shared journey.

This journey through the Three Minds is not just a story of personal growth; it is a testament to the power of resilience, empathy, and the human spirit. It is a reminder that we are all capable of great strength and compassion, both for ourselves and for each other. As we continue on this path, may we all find the courage to embrace our minds in all their complexity and beauty, and to walk together towards a future of greater understanding, healing, and shared strength.

www.ingramcontent.com/pod-product-compliance
Lightning Source LLC
Chambersburg PA
CBHW060250030426
42335CB00014B/1649